Cage of Light

ESSENTIAL POETS SERIES 295

Guernica Editions Inc. acknowledges the support of
the Canada Council for the Arts and the Ontario Arts Council.
The Ontario Arts Council is an agency of the Government of Ontario.
We acknowledge the financial support of the Government of Canada

NED BAECK

Cage
of
Light

GUERNICA
EDITIONS

TORONTO • CHICAGO • BUFFALO • LANCASTER (U.K.)
2022

Guernica Founder: Antonio D'Alfonso

Michael Mirolla, general editor
Elana Wolff, editor
Cover and Interior Design: Rafael Chimicatti
Guernica Editions Inc.
287 Templemead Drive, Hamilton (ON), Canada L8W 2W4
2250 Military Road, Tonawanda, N.Y. 14150-6000 U.S.A.
www.guernicaeditions.com

Distributors:
Independent Publishers Group (IPG)
600 North Pulaski Road, Chicago IL 60624
University of Toronto Press Distribution (UTP)
5201 Dufferin Street, Toronto (ON), Canada M3H 5T8
Gazelle Book Services
White Cross Mills, High Town, Lancaster LA1 4XS U.K.

First edition.
Printed in Canada.

Legal Deposit – Third Quarter
Library of Congress Catalog Card Number: 2021949947
Library and Archives Canada Cataloguing in Publication
Title: Cage of light / Ned Baeck.
Names: Baeck, Ned, author.
Series: Essential poets ; 295.
Description: First edition.
Series statement: Essential poets series ; 295 | Poems.
Identifiers: Canadiana 20210364351 | ISBN 9781771836999 (softcover)
Classification: LCC PS8603.A33457 C34 2022 | DDC C811/.6—dc23

Contents

for KJ
in memoriam

I didn't see one thing on my trip
but I breathed and whatever I breathed was time
       —Ikkyu

Swim and Ski Town

He helps her put clothes on.
Together they search for her shoes,
aided by the numbers—red on black—
of the alarm clock
in the dark room.

All because a human has to
get up, to up-end.

What was it then? Those days
of deep, tightly constellated trust,
fringed by nights
like pools one is punched in,
blurring the shore darker still.

He helps her because
he might come back
to hold her breasts
as if his life depended on it.

Whatever he thinks comes
like a discourteous reminder
of death in our Swim and Ski Town.

Just before he got out
the door, the make-shift curtain
(an ochre cloth)

dropped slowly from the window frame
and slid to the floor
in gold folds.

A first patch of sunlight fell across her face,
and she stared her slim watery stare,
please don't come back here.

He thought, *I wouldn't do it again*
but did. Twelve breaths.
I was thinking of apple orchards
the whole time, fields of pink-white gold
quilting the peninsula. Glass after glass
of nihilated time.

Trout Lake

October,
tracks of cold wet earth,
joggers and walkers.

A heavy, elderly woman.

Fertility, like a tortoise in the sea.
Something ponderous:
staid, slow and dexterous.

For a moment all things—
the extension of space,
swells of duration,
scattered vision
through rippling mayhem—

score on score of earthly paths,

begin, dwell and end
in her hips.

Sogenji Suite #1

We love God, just don't approve
of his lifestyle.
Between laughing at what is wicked
and having it weigh on teeth.

After vicious interludes
and interludes of peace,
after infinite days darkened by feeling
and infinite nights
streamed by thought,

Thank-you, love,
for giving birth in a rainstorm,
conceiving in a snowbank,
gestating in a skyscraper.

Thank you for running away with them—
the birds soaring over the septic system
of c-i-v-i-l-i-z-a-t-i-o-n,
strange and worthwhile.

Now take me, ticket of aloneness,
into the undivided night.

To sadness, the iron well—
put your hands around it,
it can't throw you,
it's already deeper than hell.

It may leave your body to the humours,
your sickness to the kind.

I wouldn't do it
for all the graves in Egypt.
You needn't betray yourself
for insurance.

No one is on the make here,
except the trees in the cemetery,
the devil and his people,
and the beginning of the world.

In the garden, the Roshi's fan
cools the serpent's eyes.

Around the fire,
cold night impinges
on cynic and pushover.

One reason alone
brought me here:
to get back my dream keys.

To utter an undemented no
and an economical yes.

Desire,
bird like a little fire
in the tree.

I used to get drunk
to feel like this.

Balanced by a blade of grass,
upkept by the sea.

Hieronymus Home

At sunset, a caterpillar:
wriggling butterfly machine
dances to the eyes.

Eyes,
shelter to the homeless mind.

Nations of secrecy
make a desert
of striving
that appears to stay.

Imagine its peace
and let the army do
what they're trained.

I've heard of mercy,
streets of rootless day
pass through

the face of awareness,
fielding animal dreams
turned dark, living shrieks
sinking through the dark
to a grateful Hieronymus home.

But call the light
that cures the wound of power,
surface in your parents' eyes.
Surface,
you have lived.

Alibi

The field burned at night:
small creatures, birds and insects
fled the autumn conflagration,
made for the neighbouring forest
and fence-line road.

Rain began near first light
and ended shortly after,
falling fast and in sheets.
When the flames subsided
the earth smoldered and steamed
and lay as if tamed.

Those who lit it
stared at each other with smoke-reddened eyes
across dawn's haze
and black stubble. They raised their hunted faces
to the billowing gray sky, lost
in the storm clouds, then looked down
to the remains of the harvest.

Pumpkins, corn, squash
and sunflowers left standing in the nearby garden,
downturned and dishevelled as if bearing the strain
of an alien force, rot corresponding
to a sacrifice that cannot be
absolutely completed,

but which is nonetheless responsible
for the fecundity of time
and all corruption therein.

Long ago and today, during the war in heaven,
in the guise of discorporate angels, turbid parents
grasp infants down from sun-thick fields, to taste
and be tasted by shadows.

They watch until their young sway
into youth, into that set-out darkness.

Through all of this there is
a monstrous innocence about them,
as though they are merely obeying
an energy that has galvanized
their centers, something that has closed
around the core and given them
code-words to speak.

A deranged animal innocence
in their eyes, the expectation of punishment,
just wishing to be stopped, even as they smile
and rush off to piss or shit,
when no one outside the conspiracy will touch or heed them,
when they are reminded of themselves.

The fantasy of the surface
of the sea here, to dream of love's
reprisal, an alibi
rising and falling—bodies in the waves,
though the sea is leagues and a conscience away.

I am stilled by lines whispered
from underwater places, faces once
certain to be seen.

How there is a yearning for law
in what lies down here
watching, blinking in caves
with the paintings we despise,
ear to a cold, wet wall.

Maybe we're actually to be found
under the sea's floor or a different span
of the earth, in stone crevasses
of driest ice, and only dream
of the sun
and its miscarried harvest.

Perhaps we were born
and have lived below
in a gray night
of banished coeval ideas.

To catch one's breath this time:
find one's footing
or be made to return.

Softly flooded lungs
woken in the dark, the will
to walk, to be still, to course
with singularity.

But to become the possessed
and be the possessor? Is that what their need is?
Is that what they want me to learn?

For certain there is this constraint,
a reservation like a house for all Calcutta:
the drowned and insatiable
lunge for the rising, clawing at air,
clutching at clothing, trying for flesh.

In the west garden, serried old sunflowers,
dark brown and dirty yellow on gray-green stalks
the height of a man
hang their heads—taking the shame, taking it all.
Bowing to winter to come back for them,
from the future and its atrophied tabernacle.

Thousands of kilometres and a mountain range away,
in late August, I walk along the sidewalk in a warm rain.
Past people smoking under awnings
and in doorways, knowing that
I'm alone and soaked through and well-made,
the net of time scorched and bitter
but cageless now, like rain.

Transposition

Shiny drop of water
hangs from the bathroom tap.

I see the face in reflection
unavenged, waiting
for happiness to come.

Splitting wood, emptying latrines.
Sage advice from brittle teeth,
spritely abuse in the kitchen.

There's something I'm not going to tell.
I hope you don't either.

It has to do with who saves who.

Interior

Dogs barking and sprinting,
naked December trees.

Dream hypocrisy for one
hopeful aspirant.

After exiling me, the bastard
came back in a dream, to save me
saving good Walton, knowing I couldn't.

I hope neither he nor she nor they
nor it nor any being or thing
whispers this covenant.

A Fixer's Heart

1.

Is sorrow enough to dance in the must,
in the silo with mouse droppings and furtive insects,
eerie fluttering of doves in slatted light?

Is sorrow enough to pace the damp dark,
for late thoughts,
signalling light,
action?

2.

I made it to the water today,
that is to say I bicycled south from the house
on Westmoreland, turned west on Shanly,
south on Dufferin,
west on Queen, and parked my bike at Dundas West,
where a black man in a red coat cursed
the surroundings outside McDonald's,
and two old, downtrodden men smoked marijuana
on a park bench facing Queen, and a fourth,
with unpleasant eyes,
turned to me, then gazed out
across park and highway to the water.

I walked with a dog and two tall Serbians,
a woman and man.
The woman and the dog are known to me,
the man I met for the first time.

In the dust of living
moments, there's a little room.
Discomfort and ease
in the air, with others
or alone
with light and shadow.

3.
Some pass smoothly and maybe I can offer something
to the vans of air and well-trod earth
that are their happy trajectories: printed paper, shorn hair,
the quiet of untouched blood.

Insects visit my desk: aphids, ants.
A spider does circuits of my water bottle.
My neighbour bumps against the wall.
Stoic on a spit in hell.

Occasionally I distil a good pattern,
my face lifted to the course.

A part of the mess and poison is taken away,
and the people I love,
not through death or abandonment,
but loss of self.

And I love any balm or mechanism
that allows me to exist unthreatened in space.

4.
Toward the microphone,
laughing at myself privately,
but the face is dour.

Each to and from our bodies
turn, foreheads
and eyes
turn the porous mind:

on an ice rink
playing baseball: short,
centre field, first, and pitching and umpiring too.
The catcher is cardboard with a hole
cut out for his glove.

I wish to be reborn professional,
with a fixer's heart.

5.
There's chaos in my mind,
ghosts and thoughts, whatever I don't want
I won't give to you either,
but I will give to Him, I offer them to Him, or to His Mother,
to be relieved of them,
and to the earth in its traipsing sorrow, to compost.

A maundering fat man is jealous.
A well-kempt fat woman walks gracefully
past the slow afflicted one in the park.
That's me,
across from the man with tubes in his nose,
an oxygen tank on his back.
Maybe I'll see in twenty years.

The one who prepares in language
a song sung gently at a wall,
the need that all things fall from,
as rain,
or petals.

Nights

1.
As I stood up from the mattress at dawn,
I cut my scalp on the low ceiling fan.
The others slept, drunk.
I packed and left.

Walked toward the harbour,
passed a gore of tortoise shells,
in Bluefields.

Blood and bits of flesh
from hacking and scooping
for soup; I went down to the small boats.
Took one to Little Corn Island.

I met a local man and his West Indian wife
who gave me fried food and milk,
then crossed the island and found a spot
under clacking palms in cool heat
to ease for days,
trailing thin land through trees.

Unspeaking shapes,
reliable enclosures.
Fresh oil burns
for empirical things.

2.
Late nights in
doorways
like old hands.

Now I know
five-dollar bills.
Water. I know someone brought them
because I saw them slipping away
in partial light. Their decency
here and gone.

Attempts to cast life outside
stern fault lines.

Waterline
trundling, swindling, trudging,
sweet wind.
Ships are coming, dreaming, drunk.
Full of yellow and brown and black and white.
Questing and drudgery,
each to their
materials
tightly bound.
Each triaged before the sky,
delivered by earth.

Ships are sitting in the water
loaded with goods.
Supplies for wartime peace,
hungry and scarce,
bored and immune,
wet and dry.

Looking in
to safe rooms
with clear intent.

While in the hallways
male praying mantises
who escaped the terminus
of the reproductive process
to instruct their young,
stand with clipboards,
parading visitors to patients.

If you WANT this,
arrangements can be made, financial and otherwise,
for the steady crush of days and nights
when hope will seek its only listener.

Looking in restlessness
for someone new under the sun,
some conflagration of wonder
and severance.

It often happens.
Memory finds reprieve in cinema or waiting room.
Anchored by story or pause,
dim lights in aisle stairs.

Bright eyes in dim light, there's your father,
your mother, whomever.
Until wide bare space resumes
with lights on! Lights out! The heart
an eyeless Siamese.

Be careful with threat and familiarity.

3.
The untended night movement
of a bare foot
in an unfamiliar bed,
pleased
to find nothing there.

Get up, before dread escalates
and you become occupied by the presence
of a strange place. Go.

Where?

Down the block, a Queen Street bench, 2 a.m.

A nearly empty streetcar passes
advertising the sentience
of all beings, and veganism.
It makes me think of Mike,
before he became a bastard,
the word sentience, the sword sentence, written there,
reciting Edgar Allan Poe's *Bells:*

"Keeping time, time, time,
In a sort of Runic rhyme,
To the throbbing of the bells—
Of the bells, bells, bells—
To the sobbing of the bells ..."

The walls between worlds
paper thin.

Only to Surge

I take the protestant tools laid at my feet,
and blink.

Child birth and sexual violence,
shimmering mornings.
Impulsiveness, servitude and grace
under the yellow-white
impassive moon.

Simian tools laid up in me
open my hands.

Accretion in the eyes of all creatures
twisted at full breath, salved in exhalation.

I scan, without knowing how to use,
the tools of 50 generations,
raider in my father's tomb,
and the deft cricket of the heart
idles only to surge.

Swimming for the shore
or drifting further out,
both messages arrive

and I continue to stand it—
paradise of earth and air, water and fire,
creature with a gaffed heart.

Redounding

for Yvette

The ship with the leopard flag—
I set foot on it,
and almost stayed.
I considered life there,
at ease on the sea.

The leopard flag is nearly Richard the Lionheart's flag,
nearly the flag of the Crusaders.
Returning liberators of the homeland,
friend to witches and bards,
friend to every cottage on the heath:
even the one that houses our killers;
even the one that houses our victims;
even the one that houses us,
the unbuilt ones.

I helped with the siding,
nailed a few of the deck boards in place,
and shortly after met with the octopus-man
        and the lizard-man,
who make the deals for passage and prosperity:
the octopus for the sea, the lizard for the land.

I spat in the sea, kicked at a clod of hot, dry earth
and steered away from the Bermuda Triangle.

In our port I met the Awaited and Alienated Woman,
though she was an emaciated junkie
whose breasts were a travesty
and who gave me fleas.

I met my long-lost brother, dead of brain cancer
      at age three,
who might have revealed the inception
of jet-black secrets in the family tree,
but mostly came to reduce me to dust.

To send me home, recalcitrant,
to the hayfield.
I met impassive waves, father,
and the sun shone on me
in another dimension. A cool fire
independent of the world of limbs.
I met the gold sea, mother,
in a warm, salty breeze.
To one, I loved your body as I withdrew from mine.
In your ears when no one was around
I whispered these lines:
A friend is someone you can count on for incense.
A friend is the body glowing deeper in time, whose love
      alters hell.

Weeping for a world we dreamed and destroyed,
resurrecting our love,
planting it unnoticed in another
ambient garden, to lean pure,
with as much patience as can be withstood,
behind the purple kale, next to daffodils
and a broken crock, by the folk innuendo
of second childhood, where my old friend sings and begs.

I loved watching the mischievous light in her eyes
and the way she moved. I saw her tender stomach fold
from under her shirt, and her eyes squint and gleam
when she elevated a few words of the café tune.

We drank many cups of coffee, chain-smoked
and loved one another's souls,
trawling through everything we'd done
and were doing then,
every chronicle and pore.

Now that she's gone,
a ghost goes door to door.
If you see her, care for her, as she will for you.

Because her meanness is a brick shithouse,
her delight a gold sieve,
her life spotted by disease,
and her love, her very real, tangible love
is gracious and deep
and must be upheld.

Ratio

It was the image of his
burnt face
smeared with aloe, coolant.

As a child, a hinge
of stars on dark glass
she could shatter.

Then her surprise
on an isolated beach,
thinking it was another one
fell asleep after loving her, she found
the pale, washed corpse of Icarus.
A tattoo on his inner thigh—
Ratio—faded by the sun
and sea.

Without this the cave of the world
is only the dream
of some drunkard
on a spree in the night,

crashing through windows
with the implausible grace
of dead and dying stars.

Mercy Fields

1.
The sunset sky in deep concentration
over watermelon fields.
Its colours paint as light fades.
I didn't reach today.

I rearrange my thoughts to see
if it might appear differently.
Leery of unseized day, the dark
appetitive, the senses' thieves.

Apprehension like words burnt in briar and mortar.
Plastic, paper, wood, steel and skin.
Apprehension a substratum of life,
hands thrown up, mass answers in pamphlets
proffered by hands
at the subway mouth.

A body on each side of the pamphlet-stand
in suit or skirt. Faces meander a small world,
words go up and down,
questions clothed and suffered.

Pain, lift your yellow dress.

2.
The shielding hand
twists crucially down
to the diagnostic and statistical manual.
3-dollar-bill jurist on the corner,
or the metaphysic twitch
with a panoramic view of
the widowed teat of Vancouver sky
today, to say that which is the same is different:
conscience and consciousness.
Leave the JW's alone.

There is a noise bath
on the ward and in the street,
repeated differently
after jubilation of the ill-willed
and imaginative.
Knowing full well that anyone, anywhere
unprotected from within by grace
or sleight of hand
can be rendered space-less, and be
made to row
the slave ship of space-lessness
or, as it is also known, hell.
Row if you don't, row if you know.

All this dust, perennial notes, scattered in night rain.

3.
Something occurring
unevaluated.
Something occurring:
thought, image, feeling,
make or do not make.

Night of wet watermelon fields.
Net of unspoken forms.

Maybe as we witness
the scouring of the world,
the angel, who without rank
blinks night and day,
will hold us.

To the rim of the brain
rise castles of intention,
solemn for a moment
before the swell of words.

All those years, each summer,
going to and from Eugenia beach
along the causeway,
in the back of a blue truck.
Inflatable orca
clutched and rolling in the wind.

As I, still, 30 years later, don't wake
till tomorrow midday,
when plant, animal, insect, sunlight
moan of being lost.

A hiccup of time
brings me to in the night
in this apartment on Kingsway.
Air currents through the room
where I sleep. There is something
in the walls.

Slowly turn, join
the city registry
with blurred eyes, vectors rest;
test with choice, terrorize;
offer the feline obedience
of the devil, the canine proclivity
of his messengers: part ways.

A frozen cataract spits
one of its trillion diamonds
to the door where a beggar
with a cell phone sits
long unclean. He drains black fluid
from his mouth
into a coffer, and in it
finds a precious stone.

The first few moments
of obedience and freedom.

Then perks up
for completion
of the dark arts—
steady in his pesky way—bacterial culture
keeps sickness at bay—a metaphysical distortion
that leads backward, this puppet musician
in the park, in bare feet, without instruments,
with freedom under his tongue in the form
of a sublingual focus pill.

Today was once tomorrow
before it was
our divisive goal,
our temerity to take
upon ourselves

the goat with unknown thoughts,
and no fear of the gun.

Watermelon fields, final and wet,
dancing un-culled through most of our good and our evil.

4.

They're waiting, I suspect
there's no evidence
across potential,
dwelling and exhaling,
how long it will take.

Closer and closer to an invisible seat,
hold off chin-laughter and night-contentment.

Day now, a flicker
of silver escaping
a dry torrent, looking from
stream to bank
with warm, pellucid eyes.

Caught the flesh fire many times,
was taught to throw it back, because
it always returns.

It's terrible to be taken in; to see and be cheated;
to know and disown.

5.

So the best thing
was to get drunk
and let the angel
leave the cage.

To get drunk, every day, and love
some of what loves
like everyone else.

Our heart's command
loosed fixations,
shrieked and whispered for a tunnel.

The yearning to yearn undistractedly.
To get as close
as we can, with a fierceness
unpalatable to Epicureans,
Junkets and meters of averages,
who set the rate of literate taste,
build the houses,
birth the foundlings
and confound them.

Who ogle angels
betray their friends,
and live for nothing everyday
but the saccharine grease
of evading the depths
death hides in.

warm lead
dropped in watermelon fields
at night, in the rain

cries overhead, bright sun
diving crows,

listening at night, bright sun
fields under rain,
everything waiting for passage

this is the peace of the real
boy and sick kid
ambivalent mother and gun
warm lead

6.
Those wary
of betraying space
take upon
themselves
a great danger.

Unborn love at work in their veins.
The river of mind in each eviscerated
wing, to call out form
kingfishing our eyes.

I grew up and moved away to a bridal city. I hoped
no animal dream would follow me here.
If it did, despite my efforts, I prayed

to be
led to the
pit of my gut.

The hand in a fist
against the pew,
prayer book stropped-
mind crossed in the ceiling.

I can't see.
Am barely accustomed
to anger bent double,
and the scent of dead wind
from the alps,
         but transmute pain,
or abdicate?

Wandering the watermelon fields at night
looking for the centre of the same light,
falling and being rained on,
each spacious drop.

To stop those bullets you chose for me,
though you didn't bother to shoot them.
Dreams can be that bright.

Dreams born in the night
but conceived
somewhere else.

Gathered and regathered.

Somewhere we cannot help
but find.

Outside-In

Damp papers mouldering in the street,
pages slowly flipped by a wet mid-winter breeze.

Linked but not as things
to sunlight's shot at the moon, animals crossing
a footpath, civic morass, no recourse before the sky.

It's not whether you're counted
or still counting impingements,
or to give up
the goodness of rest, the brain
your mind is a child in.

But to go back
through name and time,
passed what agent memory finds
in likeness and discomfort,
for a while ...

Then you're back where what crushed
is shrugged off like it's death camp.
One mutiny after another,
weight thrown around
for a defiant muse.

Because it's partially real, the losing land,
secession and hindsight.

Eyes sunk back in sockets
like embers burrowing
into Persian rugs,
fixed in ornate links.

Scenes of light and dark
inoculate prejudice,
the degeneracies of life
being ours
until we step from the myth
but keep our passports.

The child is born perfect, if it's born at all,
screaming in the straw and clay.
The source-world delivers
without seams or assurance,
and time congeals,
its lone provision.

Compelled first to anguish and then gradually
to attention through the cringing hours.
The available milk, the warmth,
the promise of faces and voices.

Still, humanity with its age-old tactic circles,
strives, voluntarily drowns then burns itself alive,
drunk on symbols and magical formulae
for milk, infallible food, the promise of faces
and voices, the working of hands.

He Served in the Court
of the Empress Seville

across the lake from Sheba.
He brought her his shambles and the evening till.
Highwaymen looked coldly at his passing form,
children mocked his old, uncovered name.

He thought *what am I doing?*
as he sewed her clothes.
He thought *I am dismaying*
the stones and the hills.
I am displaying rudimentary consciousness.

The vagrant moon
cast him a violent, purple look.

Where does treason go?
It repairs the hearts of enemies
and seals the lips
of estuaries, where seagulls spin
their angled shapes
over stranded minnows,
and time escapes.

The purple curtain,
with its treasured ungodliness,
is next year's choice
of shoes,

so scars are trodden
into oblivion by infants.

A glint of shamelessness
in the smiles of snuffed lives
is passed over by a barista,
and lingers in birdcalls
as snow settles
on a thin grey tree.

By a stream forded at the onset
of pitch-coloured pig-dogs
popular on iPhone,
its banks glowing with earth's
restrooms.

He who loses his enemy loses his treasure,
he who balks at transcendence
shuffles up the street at noon.

He wept once on a long flight.
Loved beautiful, violent women,
superlative, superfluous.

He auditioned for an opera about ransom,
drank Gatorade from a gallon jug,

and ran at the sphinx.
Someone slipped him a pill.

He expunged a gamey pheasant
from the underbrush
where another lay drunk.

He even took his hand, he even helped him stand up
and accompanied him to the bible store.
The man in the dream asked him
Do you have the humility to save us?
He trusted him.
Did he have the temerity?
He had the infirmity.

Did he? He lacked harshness
and more than that he lacked
forbearance and planning.

Sheba killed the empress,
lauded him some hard knocks,
but always showed up his devastation
with maidens.

She told him to become his problems,
become his enemies,

then he wouldn't have any.
He would have the peace of reckless cessation,
and live on lordly grease and imaginary eddies
and her favour.

He had to get out of the birdbath all at once,
every time he fell in.
The balcony over the garden was leaning
and could collapse on young children
playing below at any time.
In the dead of night,
the heart of day,
in small hours of averted life.

Everything is okay,
love is any agreement.
If the water runs out,
you can drink shampoo.
Since nobody comes,
nobody leaves.

You can do something with your bodies if you want to,
for nowhere in the sky is there anything more.
Nobody will cry out
except the apprentices at the psych ward,
and only the first few times.

I am he, and despite
these dreary untruths,
somehow I still want you
to be here, not just you, a true lover
or friend.

I wasn't tough to deepen,
despite my blood-red failures
and the glue in my eyes.

Or I mean I want to be here
still moved, un-indifferent
to the pain that makes money,
and would like to counteract,
cast a ribald glance at squirrels,
walk gallantly to the park
to perform my daily ablutions.

Wishing to be caressed or assessed
by certain humans,
cordial to the maw,
and completely ignored by others.

Keep the wine near at hand,
we have to work early.
There is a spine tree,

you only get one per capita.
All bending, abdication and horse-eating
    are preapproved.
You did what? We have a place for you.
Lastima, que lastima.
Quid pro quo.

To the league against recalcitrance
and horsehair hovering
over the evil thing,
whatever human filament of degradation
you're linked to, I vow to do the cleaning myself,
with some help.

A silkworm for the hawk,
a footpath for the dew
when summer comes.

Backyard, 3 p.m.

I see breeze in the tree,
and sunlight.

I meet them underground,
chafed and abbreviated,
a lasting host for killer bees.

Eventual to time unchosen,
overlapping minds,
tides and estuaries.

Where are you?
I know where you are,
you're always there, aren't you?
Waiting just beyond
an aura of bad faith,
waiting for me to relinquish
this hide-bound thing.

I waited for the thief to catch me up,
pressed a leaf into his hand,
helped remove pebbles from his shoes.

Ran five miles to greet a dilettante,
then lay down hoping for cessation.

Most gods,
in civil altercation,.
begged me to move on.
Too much enemy smoke.

I need a motorbike or a gun.
Profiles of enmity, dimensions developed
in an effort to wield my own.

So I sit down here,
and the devils sit down over there—
all arrayed in a house of being.

I'm still now,
here
with my correctional facility mistakes,
and you arrive, eyes thatched with pain, a dying animal,
with a bottle under your coat.

The night will visit soon, draw our length into its liquid
        embrace,
psyche active, indisposed,
there will be a chance.

Who dreamt torture for decades,
I begin to see,
what matters to the masters
is difficulty rising in the morning.

To the masters
of spring and fall jackets,
city lights so free,
what matters
is a shed made into a chicken coop.

What about the rocks at the bottom of a lake,
not going any deeper.
And pebbles shifting
and shifting against each other
until they're sand.

If the only thing were to not blame others.

Patience, patience
said the quiet voice
without a world.

Essai

What did you see? The devil's tears.
(Dry sunlight cannot dry them.)
You should've run.

The circumstance of life:
perpetual deliverance
and the shadow's retaliation,
perpetual.

Spine climbing
sun snake,
our skin clothes oily bright.

Is one of them
if turned into listener,

perpetual.
Is it not your job,

would a different mind have waded
when blood reddened the stream?

Perpetual,
the dark ones
consider faith
a dependency
to be cured.

Won't talk,
walk away
down a beige dirt road
and follow,
answering gentleness
offensiveness,
harshly dispatch.

Seeing this
guts sing,
brain rings.

We can be brought from this world.
Perpetual sync,
perpetual Inc.
Lean against the car
at night,
overlook the town.

Light in spades.
You've always looked into the dark.
Traffic gone to bed.
Children imagine,
safe from conception,
their astonished hearts
not yet.

Gently they regard a spider,
assuming nothing,
just wondering.

Perpetual
thank-you.
It would be alright if that were the only prayer.

Ghosts

X means nullity, O, submission.
There's a transatlantic to the river Aaron,
but what we're treating here
is the transatlantic to the river Abel
and then on to the river Seth.

It was during layover that murder occurred:
sacrifice, preference, envy.
Even then, events are unwound,
causes dissolved, and time ushered away.

The clutched stone recoiled from the brow,
its breakage healed,
the skin of the forehead smoothed back to the skull.
(It's similar to the burning house we must be tricked
    to leave.
You have to rest in the light like a surrendered gun.)

And since any sincere offering is the best offering,
the world of ingratitude, uprooting of seed,
is merely one potential realm
in the infinite connective
of loosely drawn plans.
The teachings pass down
that *we know this, we do this* ...
but many of us return to a house
covered in flames, undress,
and drop into bed, finished.

There's no last word in ambiguity, so we're forgiven
before we begin.
(Though do you prefer to be chastened,
and marked, or unwritten?)
It's difficult to live in a God of real-time myth
and actual cosmogony. The faintest whisper worth
more than reams of glorious army
shod in titanium sitting down
to feast on grief's extinction.

Call them haunted, they are merely laws.
I want to follow them.

Pocket to the Milky Way

I'm not the expert.
I don't draw on dew cushions
or kick at the coroner.
Don't waste makeup on my corpse.

Tongues yawn in vain.
Bodies shuffle and huff,
slip equine to the street,
to paw the ground and chortle.

I wasn't made for this,
plangent hands around the throat
of illness, to pass fraternally
the mock-up victories
of the deceased-to-life.

I sit, in this day
of 40 years,
a benchmark to the foetus,
an ash mark on the wall.
This much I've shrunk,
this much grown.

*

Atlas plays cards with a shark.
It deserves saying how hard it is
for Atlas to remain Atlas

and the shark to remain the shark.
Moss grows around the elbow,
blue in the hand.

For the game to be played,
for light not to slip
into darkness, darkness
to light, for each card to stand
for itself alone: Jack of Diamonds,
Ace of Hearts,
Queen of Spades.

*

I'm homeless in this house,
and worse, I'm eavesdropped.

Listen to eyes,
the heath and hearth in them.
Keep this prayer,
utter it
in a deaf roar—
to arms of safety,
on some cool night
below the moon.

*

I left home of my own volition
and by necessity; there was no difference.
It's the action in doubt that kills,
against the weights of forbearance.

Brutal hands reach for juvenescence,
but whose are they? No one knows.
There's too much faith, too much betrayal
to determine that.

Who will teach winter to summer?
All hearts alight, Let me, let me.
Woe to those perfect August nights
of January.

*

Beach abandoned and full of bottles,
the deck burned to ashes,
ash marked on the wall.
Precisely rubbed into the off-white
half-way through life, left standing
with nothing in the heart
but a sleepless child.

Blackened jacks take the place
of crisp laminate,

ready hands and nursed beer
of floating summers.

Children cheated on, family and spouse.
It's not enough to wish,
it's not enough to be good.

You have to grind pavement into dust
with dedication.
March backward
into the chrysalis,
forehead burning.

How can you wish well of feigned appetites?
How can you wish well of cut corners?
The cruel decencies of faith you keep?

*

I remember swollen breasts in early motherhood.
Gladness at the stamina of the early days.
I remember hating you because you were wet
and witness to my fear,
the only witness left.

I awoke today from transvestites on airplanes,
    each saying

through thickly arranged lips, I'm a man,
one by one, I'm a man.

I got up in other words to dreams, my dreams,
sent or generated, that wash through the open gates
of a porous mind, remnants of another day, another town
washed away.

*

A decision to walk on one side of the street,
to cross over and cross back.

To work and moan,
dreading wickedness in life.

Gaze at a moment's portal
in hands that make change, beginning
in bottomless and realizable need
of lungs, belly, eyes,
the brain stem
shot right through the neck of a lizard
into the pocket of the Milky Way.

*

A wolf swallows
your evening
and morning star,
shudders and crawls
to a van, as into the clean hands of a thief,
an arrow in its chest.

Into the wizened hands of an infant,
neglected and searching.
To keep you scared. To keep you
scarred and longing
in this longing, this thief-stem of the conscious world,
revolving in a can of garbanzo beans
for a dollar and 69 cents.

Life Is Chastened

As a well by dryness
or a forest by fire.
A well or forest
by silence—

the other welcoming
committee
welcome
to its own
dark
feats.

Boss of the ambidextrous,
rigour of two bodies
painting each other blue.

South as it leans into north,
north in its upright gyre.

Chastened by threat of hell,
balls to the wall.
Waiting to coach a burning Frisbee,
waiting to inhale fire.

Waiting to be there
when the reptile brain reviles heaven and earth,
and the white-touched sea is beaten with rods.

Sating the air
with breath, the body
with flesh, the mind
with space, the undressed
with proficiency. Shriving
absolutely. Soap on dirty skin.

Rugged as a house for the drifter,
Serengeti answered in the zoo:
daemon evolution, beautiful kid
saved from harm by its dutiful parent,
guardian and protector of the mind.

A minnow escaping
the high-bound secrecy,
clean blood preventing
dissolution of the psyche.
Hands fleeing themselves, lifting up.

Initially the
flood rose out of love.
The body had been
consumed by fire.

The one for whom it counted,
the aspiration of woman and man,
their child bore that fire.

Inverted order backpedalling
into desire
with urgent, restorative sadness
of a drunk in a fountain.

The dove drowning in remembered eyes
and the sea-monster that saved it
in foreseen ones.

Souls

Seek the near names.
Night air on balcony, love
for the middle of night.

Deathless and deathful
stars, *worlds, words.*
Whose idea,
whose seeing is this?

It's too lit up here.
Too bright
To see the sky's black
mouthful of diamonds.

This yearning,
this cooling
breeze in the night.

This burning,
this soothing.
These coals
in the gut
reign.

Crooked Link to Perfect Night

The intellect is, within a certain focus,
past a certain point, stateless.

I don't admire it much,
but because I entrust myself to her, I imagine
asking her if she's crazy, like the beauty
of electrical equipment on a telephone pole
in the night-lit alley, crazy like a fox with a metal brain.

I woke up wearing shoes.
There's a lot to do before entering the world
of pizza and busses and fence posts,
of beaten mothers and banks,
by way of secret underground streams
through certain white-eyed nights.
Violent, still and full. One pearl

of wisdom is such an eye
retrieved from the psychic swamp,
the 'oyster' losing its name
to ensconced surrounding humus
and baked into inedible bread.
There is a lot to do before the huge battery
of the mental heart
eats that bread and dies to current forms.

For the unfilled noose,
the rotting but somehow always fresh
cornucopia of freedom,
during the tranquil period
of an infinite look.

Draw oxygen from the pool
of atmosphere,
scoop with its lungs
the night houses' yellow eyes
and those lives behind them
with their plants and pets.

Humans sleep or watch
TV in East Vancouver night,
stereoscopic minds
cleanse the city's masterwork adults,
who chant inside-out,
You'll die
and you can't,
not of tree-processed air,
not of the unexplained world
to which tree-branches belong,
which humans turn to enjoy.

Branches slowly
sprouting leaves and perches.
But if you should end there,
grip the air
with your feet, go up
when the jolt grips your neck.
Hover, turn out the victim
from sarcophagus skin,
placate the energy
of trapped incarnation,
incanted despair.

Don't mind the meat, it'll waste and idle
and float like a white moon below the stair
in the shadow lair
of delusion
inside us all.

Take care, we're going to die now
and sleep comfortably
through the involuntary consciousness of depravity
for the rest of our lives.

Grays, reds and blacks
in grays, reds and blacks
from under stripped material
poke our empty heads.

Rest on rock-hard pillows,
industrial-strength shadows
below a kilometre of evening
crows. I stand to see, breathing
consciously or without parentage.

Folding each day into its trivial
and going home inches away,
when objects are allowed
to nourish themselves,
and shadows turn
to burning trees.

And discuss what? Ideas and disease.

A scented knife in the chest
like a cat
in the night-house,

looking up at the balcony and starlight,
to the probability of scraps in the garbage,
and across the alley to me,

where I love her.

What Are We Talking

and shouldering,
what thoughts and what thinking?
Relief, you think
is relief from breathing
but it's the relief of breathing
without self-borne thought. You shouldn't ask
for too many things or the asking
gets confused. Ask for

one
free (from)
thought,
ask
for
nothing—
the garbage
in the road,
the impossible
traffic
like reams of birds,
sunset and the damage of a body,
tumours of thought,
stealth of joy
and violence under the visible disc
of the sun,
phantoms, phantoms and bent light,
Vesuvius dawn

and her thespians—
you can hear her thighs
cringing
in the stillness of the empty park
on top of the pond,
the sound of gravel
shovelled
into the sea
like imagined love,

(on a disgruntled night
by the sea)

snow more delicate than rain
falling into its surface,
settling on my hands.

Crow

Pistons ever-ready.
Crow on a black slanting roof
carries a leaf, hops midway up.
Somewhere a lanky woman
is thanking me.

Innocent

What do we
make,
what mistake?

Disturbed by sunlight when it falls
on the creatures who maraud at night,
as they hide or manoeuvre through day.

It's strange that the danger is seen to be
in illumination, from which hearths are built,
while the draggled wounded ride
the alleys of the mind,
shielded from eyes,
protracting the causes of pain.

Let's speak on the level
till the day-and-night earth
is home.

Not delay the unpolished sounds of grace
as it gathers, a little light raised
to clean sight, trees, a woman entering
a park from the street,
a toddler wandering.

Evening colours will flush again
and light be soft and deep.

I'm among the wounded and compromised,
and know the stable is full of good horses
even I can ride.

They sleep on good straw,
hear the birds,
see the light change as we do.

Their minds and hearts
as amenable as ours to this
concoction of pain and avidity.

Section House

1.
Though bevelled,
conscience keeps us hopeful.

We speak, walk the street,
carry out our days. The wind,
undarkened,
checks our resignations

through more than one season, with logic
for each calloused interior,
and for ointment,
        a moneyed smile.

In moments, wavering roots
of a luminous plant
lost in the night
of the city aquifer.

2.
In the house, ghosts
climb the stairs, ensconce
objects with vacuous eyes,
in their effort to flee,
colonize.

Maybe it isn't captivity,
but the senses' slow infidelity
to time, passing reality
like a candy wrapper
kept in a pocket,
pressed tight against the back of a hand,
or clenched and let go.

Allusions for the atrium
loaded on a bus.

Apocryphal moments
kept still in the current.

Yearning for victory
over small tyrannies,
reprieve,
early mastery,
the attic tenant rushes out.

3.
Halted by egregious thoughts
at the bridge to the lakeshore,
for a moment considering thighs,
people with strong hearts
shaped by pain and incongruency.

Loners in bamboo clothing
driving wicker jeeps
into the clouds.

Dear world,
viscid extension,
hedge, vow.
Anguish changes

as light changes,
fading
to where dark tenders
a circle,
and the waterline.

4.
Martine drove me to my rented room,
our hands clasped over the gear shift.

(That morning, she had come into the guestroom,
lain at my side, breathed softly on my face.)

Outside, young Hasids smoked in alleys,
ushering me from her warmth
to what waited:
the dear smoothness and depth of alcohol.

She was always saying
Can't your father help you,
I was always saying
No.

A year later, a year ago,
I was sobbing in a vacant factory with an old friend.

Just before, in the street, to passers-by,
He's alright. Fried potatoes in a wok,
loses his keys so he keeps
the window open, whatever the season.

Also, he likes the air.

5.
One morning, Loki tried to steal my pants off the floor,
with a branch, perched on the fire escape.
I heard change clinking in the pockets in my dream
and woke and said, What are you doing?
He shucked them off the branch and said,
Sorry, I'm very high,
and slowly retreated.

I saw him in the streets a day later
and that was when he told me his name was Loki.
We spoke, comrades in on an old joke.

My nose was bleeding daily, when not at home
I was in bars,
my head cramped under a faucet.

Martine called me from her cell phone
New Year's Eve. She was cross-country skiing
somewhere in Quebec. When I listened to the voicemail
I heard love in her words,
and laboured breathing.

After long absence I missed her voice.
I wrote,
and she wrote back:
　There is no doubt I do not wish to mingle.
　I only want you as a shadow
　in my backpack.

6.
A good sunset now.
Bleeding cattle seen from a train window,
red smears across their flanks
on the deep lake. Near-dark, near-forgiving,
near sleep.

We are alone enough,
whatever we comprise.
Reaching, meeting, clasping,
a separate pair in each other's eyes.

Strong and plain when the sun returns,
lighting house and tree, a child,
man dancing down the street,
his shadow.

The Persistent Light of the Moon Indoors

Don't you know it's a courtesy time conducts?

High on mushrooms, pot and beer,
I sat with Nick Barbuto, against the fence,
under the bleachers, as the cops viewed
the park, we not too afraid, imagining
at blank range the possibilities.

And they were: evening hijacked,
a short visit to a holding cell
and a call to each of our homes,
contrite and laughing early nights,
or by virtue of threat vanishing
from overactive imagination,
continuing on to the high school dance
where we'd trip on strobes and music.

Memory over.
I get to the café 25 years later,
held together by a small wish.
I order coffee, a microbial shape
passes through my vision,
I think it's falling from the ceiling,
and wave my hand in front of my face,
it's just my eyes.
The persistent light
of the moon indoors.

About current predicament,
utter not a word
of wheat vs chaff,
to exeunt the wrong pile.

Stand up adroitly and step, or roll,
across the near floor, and embed
in the right heap.

The mystery will sieve you plentifully
with golden flax, your cup running over.

Do you think I'm doing a good job?
asks each babe in a litter of bats,
but the mother is out sucking fruit
or cow, and can't answer right now.

You'll find yours soon,
and lose it, and go on trying to find it forever.

Still on the Ocean

Symbols drawn in alley.
Refuse and clean colours
from trees—scent of eschaton,
effluence of Thursday—never mind, empty plastic
bag glided by meandering airs
across the street last night—and now
the phone rings.

With talk at first engaged then slinking,
with footsteps of little rabbits sniffing,
words from nests lowered from living current
into an apartment to soften the urgency of eyes,
dissolve the scowling shrine
and replace it with dead lazy afternoons,
sipping evening. If you look for enemies
hovering, ingratiated ones linger, gathering
flints of awareness in triage.

Basic assessment—failure to cope.
Carried out mostly by sitting casually but upright
on chairs, in jaws—as I see it—of civilized compromise.
Jaws. Flints shine
from faults where psychic spaces rise. They're
     sequestered.
Well, the room isn't mine. I never said it was.
Just listen a bit longer to little rabbits sniffing,
word-order emptied from nests
brought to the lap of the hospital.

I swam once at Wreck Beach. The coast guard came.
We were all glowing phosphorescent from the water
and high
from sand cliffs we jumped from to get down there.

I ask no questions and reply enough.
A wound is suddenly clean before it changes.
Instantly charged among
blood-drawing instruments and clipboards and
identity bracelets.
Faultline among the ambulatory, troubled people
in varying degrees of health. Not indissoluble
    but indivisible.

The hospital is at root a cluster of sonic frequencies.
For warped or nearly broken units who are at root peace
tenured by clan destiny.

Go back to the tribes through tubes,
clipped hair,
womanly-filled unisex scrubs.

Thin cheese sandwiches slowly eaten,
summoning tact.
Infrastructure of respite,
shiny doctor dealing
certain kinds of helpful death.

This is more one-time-running episode of survival
or psychic sling.

Affix the ramrod spine.
Take in the slid-up gold anklets of an old woman
folded into a stretcher, all dignity and decency.
It's okay here, you see me, we are all still
on the ocean here, in a boat of tremendous elasticity,
and the mind is
roughly like the brain.

Dark Blue Grass

There is a bird in
my eye in
my skull in
my chest in
a tear drop in
the violence of
this world that
countenances and
confounds loss there
is a bird there
is flight without
content in
my pupil in
the contracted darkness in
the cave of my
heart there is
a bird knowing
was in the
confusion where the
sacred body stumbled into
cold stone on
the beach on
the Newfoundland coast where
I was drunk through
the night with the
others and
found myself on

a boulder a
way's off at
dawn waking up, not
knowing how
long I'd
been sleeping the
sound of waves breaking the
others still gathered still
talking in the
dawn light but
quieter now the
ether wearing
off, drifting
still awake faces
drained eyes
wan Julia was
there we
held hands as
we walked back to
the house there was
moisture in the
dark blue grass it
brushed against
our legs as
we walked

Imagine Us Watching the Sky for Birds

When I'm with you I feel at home,
time slips
to the tensionless earth;

try to sit up but see the old goof
up to his tricks again;
see I've rigged the effort
to reach spirit, scatter need.

Hide treasure in the bitter ease
of switchgrass, the trace of life
where a deer has lain.

We'll be together again
X-rayed in the garden,
see each other's infrastructures
and through those unmoved
the secret taste
of avowal.

Imagine us watching the sky for birds,
sensing something vacant
in our sturdy shoes.
With hearts that bray
for silence, wanting to know.

The new defense for abdication—
something deeper than god
can't be betrayed,
is deeply betrayed,
profaned, astonished by the sanctimonious.

Drained, empty for a moment,
but soon pleasure and displeasure fill the eye
and we are in the round.

Desire is not a prison if bounded by the impersonal,
neither is anger,
I want to know your pain—

when the tenure of shadow constricts,
but you throw it off,
when the labile pressure of shadow
dumbfounds and indicts
the deck of this boat,
but you shake it off.

We're together
in the trachea of the cosmos.
Song rising, then bile;
chase each other
demanding approval.
Successful in pain
to be successful at something.

We are here privately on this boat.
One day it doesn't need to be rowed,
it's lotus or water lily.
Redemptive, our karma the best luck,
depending on how it's said.
If it hides something, row.

Row. I don't know
the way back or the way
forward, though sometimes it goes
inward, moves to still,
gently, safely. Shudders.
For all our animal pain
someday we'll turn inside.

To leaves plastered on sidewalks,
wet earth and ochre. The business
of streets closing for the night,
opening to something else.

Beyond our effort to depart.

Throughout earth, throughout our wishing hearts
we shouldn't stay too long
or it undoes us, as if it doesn't want to be happy,
as if it is.

Sogenji Suite #2

Rusty, bent angles
of bicycles
left to the streets.

The sun streams on.

*

Something stands up
when I want to fall down,
raking sand,
crows shifting through the graveyard.

Apart from Zazen, chanting,
grounds work and formal meals,
I move for coffee and chocolate
along the alleys of Okayama.

Sun and shadow-striped, barking dogs
never seen, slow moving
turtles glint in the canals,
one dead in a yellow pond.

Different shades of birds sing at night,
and it pours during *yaza*,
enveloping the stillness
and making insects sultry.

*

Seated outside the scripture hall, sheltered by eaves,
footsteps and someone
appearing from Mountain Gate
with a blanket and an umbrella.

It takes a long time
and then you see it,
the black sun.

It's not that you can't count on it,
you just can't take
mosquito coils
for granted.
Can I talk to you?
He's sitting at the corner of the building,
half-enclosed.

As the hours turn into seconds
where air meets the brain,
primitive indecencies,
occasionally a lover's eyes.

Flesh, snakes, birds,
mer-people
clutching conches and draped in seaweed.
Dark, unknown song of air.

Cleans the mind,
gives day to day
and night to night.

*

An unreconciled man told me
we sleep in the dark
and walk in the light.

He wanted praise for his conclusions
and a hiding place for his shame.

No single leaf or blade of grass would change.

The forest spirits aren't in the woods surrounding
Sogenji tonight, my eyes aren't at risk in the dark.

Go back to the river, ravenous energy.

There's nothing beyond the wall of rain.
Listen to the droplets and feel the wet night air.
It's getting late.
Morning bell in 4 hours.

Through the Waves

I miss them as quick, pained, intelligent children.
I don't miss them as them tawdry, disingenuous adults.

Something occurs that is devastating
to anyone who cares.

Disappear below the waves,
bare warmth
to bare coolness.

Disappear perfectly.
Sink slowly through the waves
like a bleached skeleton.
So very, very
drily,
even
when wet,
through the bottomless
reek of sea, and stay.

With the recorded inaction
of power and
silence.

Unbroken alembics,
innocent of eyes.

Triggered in Your Cradle

Yawns and imprecations breed in the midden
running through and pooling every day.

The sun like a radiant mountain looks on us,
finds us at a storefront, in the gutter by the coffee cup.

Finds us shrilly crossing the street,
going somewhere to properly despair
of oxygen with a straight back.

Snaps its golden fingers and fills its bellows
with nutriment and heat.
Yin and yang, these are things you must contend with.

Come, to heal you have to
go back and forth.

A rhododendron
and a deep, white flower, floating
in a summer night.

Drank rain from it, autumn, spring
and winter that it hurts to breathe,
the most desolate,
the most devious, the most natural
of humans.

Raise your hands, focus your eyes,
there are going to be more
impulses and reasons
rife with pain and love and obligation.

The most vulnerable of creatures,
slugs, all over the lawn.

You are still in that state,
still unhoused,
triggered in your cradle.

Those empty ears and frightened heart
and something else
listens.

Words from a Dream

I was hazy. Drunk again,
unable to tell how old people were.
You never talk about your parents, Tyler said,
I guess you don't care about them.
I don't care about anyone, I said.
You're not any more drunk than usual, my mother said,
but you're more incoherent.
And clean up your room for once, like Liane does.

Someone came into the kitchen
for the purpose of looking at my drunkenness,
my dishevelment.
I asked Tyler to stop assembling his meal
of sunflower seeds
and have a sequestered talk.

They rape and are emboldened, I said.
Oh, I haven't learned that Japanese art.
Adam and Eve stood straight, he said.

we live in a cage of light an amazing cage
animals animals without end
        —Ikkyu

Notes

The epigraphs are from *Crow with No Mouth*, by 15th century Zen Master, poet and calligrapher Ikkyu, translation by Stephen Berg, Copper Canyon Press, 1989:25;55.

He Served in the Court of the Empress Seville: "He who loses his enemy loses his treasure" is a paraphrase of a line in Lao-Tzu's *Taoteching*. The actual line, "to have no enemy is to lose one's treasure," can be found in the translation by Red Pine, Copper Canyon Press, 2009:138.
"Superlative, superfluous" is delivered by Al Pacino in the film, *Scent of a Woman.*

What Are We Talking: The line "what thoughts and what thinking?" echoes the following line from *A Game of Chess*, part II of T.S. Eliot's *THE WASTE LAND*: "What are you thinking of? What thinking? What? (T.S. Eliot, *Selected Poems*, Faber and Faber, first published 1954:55.)

I realize now I unconsciously quoted Bob Dylan in the poem "Life is Chastened". In "Chimes of Freedom," he sings of the 'guardians and protectors of the mind.' Mine is in the singular, 'guardian and protector of the mind.'

Acknowledgements

I wish to thank the editors of the following publications in which poems in this collection first appeared:

The Continuist: "Dark Blue Grass"
The Nashwaak Review: "Outside-In"
Poetry Pause: "Ratio"

I extend thanks to Betty Brown and Djamel Hamdad for ongoing dialogues, they are life-sustaining.

Thanks to the people and premises of Sogenji Temple in Okayama, Japan, where I trained for five months in 2019; to Daichi Zenni for allowing me to come, for counsel and guidance, and for arranging medical support during my stay; to Harada Roshi for exemplifying the Zen spirit and leading through all aspects of practice; to the sangha for their patience and camaraderie.

Thanks to Matthew Herschler for offering early editorial help on "Section House" and again to Betty Brown for early editorial help with "Backyard, 3 p.m.," as well as advice as I worked to convey salient words about the collection; to Luciano Iacobelli and Claudio Gaudio for maintained friendship and artistic alliance; to Dobrila Tomic and Mia for many walks and conversations. It didn't end well, but we had a good run; to John Dumbrille and Michelle Meyrink, newfound allies; to John Fox for friendship and for storing my belongings when I left for Japan, shipping them to me in Toronto, and then ungrudgingly welcoming me back to Vancouver.

Thanks to Guernica Editions publishers Connie McParland and Michael Mirolla, who accepted this second manuscript, and to Michael in particular, who has been even-keeled and helpful during the creation of this book. I am glad to have worked again with Elana Wolff as editor: we've developed a rapport beyond the poetry and I trust her guidance.

Thanks to Rafael Chimicatti for his resourcefulness and ingenuity in design.

Thanks again to Luciano Iacobelli and also to Shazia Hafiz Ramji for agreeing to read a late iteration of the unpublished manuscript and write something about the book.

About the Author

Cage of Light is Ned Baeck's second full-length collection of poems with Guernica Editions. (His first collection, *Wait*, was released in 2018.) He is also the author of a chapbook with LyricalMyrical press. Baeck studied Liberal Arts at Concordia University and Asian Studies at the University of British Columbia. He has lived for most of the last twenty years in Vancouver.

Printed in May 2022
by Gauvin Press,
Gatineau, Québec